I0236189

junkyard wisdom advent

AUTHENTIC, DAILY DEVOTIONS ABOUT THE HUMAN, HUMOROUS, AND SOMETIMES MESSY SIDE OF THE ADVENT STORY

ROY GOBLE

with **D. R. JACOBSEN**

FIRST SILVER THREAD PUBLISHING EDITION, SEPTEMBER 2024
All rights reserved. No part of this book may be reproduced, scanned, or distributed in
any printed or electronic form without explicit written permission.
Silver Thread Publishing is a division of A Silver Thread, Arroyo Grande, CA
www.asilverthread.com
Content Copyright © 2024 by Roy Goble
Junkyard Wisdom™
All Scripture quotations, unless otherwise noted, are taken from
THE HOLY BIBLE NEW INTERNATIONAL VERSION
Copyright © 1973, 1978, 1984, 2011 by Biblica, Inc.
Used by permission. All rights reserved worldwide.
Paperback Version ISBN 978-1-7353845-5-9
Hardback Gift Edition ISBN 978-1-7353845-6-6
Printed in the United States of America

Endorsements

"If you're like me, you want more Christ and less craziness in your Christmas. This Christmas, I'll be re-reading these fresh devotions by Roy Goble. Each one is short, pithy, and practical, with a few poignant reflection questions that further deepen their impact. Most importantly, they creatively explore Mary and Joseph's experiences and emotions leading up to Jesus' birth so that the life-changing meaning of that birth becomes more powerful during Advent, and all year long."
KARA POWELL, PHD, CHIEF OF LEADERSHIP FORMATION AT FULLER SEMINARY AND CO-AUTHOR OF *FAITH BEYOND YOUTH GROUP*

"In this captivating devotional, Roy Goble takes us on a road trip with Mary and Joseph, inviting us deeper into the Advent story. It is funny, spiritually insightful, and extremely relevant for people who want to grow closer to the God who became human like us. I loved it and highly recommend it!"
DR. BRENDA SALTER MCNEIL, AUTHOR OF *EMPOWERED TO REPAIR AND BECOMING BRAVE*

"Roy's Advent meditations are a new invitation to draw closer to the rugged, often chaotic days leading up to Christ's birth. He brings us far closer to the human experience, and in doing so, we draw near to the holy ground of anticipation. Light breaks through, in the most unexpected ways. Keep this book close for all of your Advents to come." AMY LOW, MANAGING DIRECTOR OF EMERSON COLLECTIVE, AUTHOR OF *THE BRAVE IN-BETWEEN*

"These Junkyard Wisdom Advent devotions are a delightful mix of scripture, curiosity, and celebration. Each daily reading encourages the reader to wrap faith around the days leading up to Christmas. It's a fresh way to open the month of December, adding joy and wonder to your Christmas tradition."
DEBBIE ALSDORF, AUTHOR OF *10 MINUTES WITH GOD FOR WOMEN, THE FAITH DARE, AND DEEPER*

Who says humor is irreverent?! Roy Goble wraps wit, warmth, and wisdom into a wonderfully winsome Advent experience. I laughed, even as I rediscovered the awe surrounding the birth of Christ. I've been in ministry for over thirty years, yet I found these devotions both insightful and delightful. Perfect for any reader to enjoy. LAKITA WRIGHT, MEDIA CONSULTANT, SPEAKER, AND AUTHOR OF *THE NAKED TRUTH*.

"If you think you know the Christmas story, think again! Roy delights his readers by telling this age-old story through an imaginative lens with a lot of sass thrown in. Roy uses humor and hyperbole to help us look between the lines and picture what was said and done. I found myself smiling on every page! Roy makes the Advent story more than a staid vignette on a Christmas card by taking us into a human story, raw and vulnerable, where we might find ourselves as fellow travelers. Experience Advent in a fun, fresh way and find yourself falling in love with the Christmas story all over again!" EMILY NELSON, CO-FOUNDER OF THE FLOURISH COLLECTIVE

"I love how the author incorporates sarcasm." MARY MAGDALENE

Table of Contents

Dedication

For Lillian Rose.

*May the hope, peace, joy, and love of Christmas
always delight the child in you.*

Our Journey Begins

ARE YOU PACKED AND READY TO GO?

Tomorrow is the big day when we can finally start eating our chocolate Advent calendars! Well, it is if you happened to open this book on the Saturday before the fourth Sunday before Christmas, or something like that. Confused? Me too. The early church leaders, God bless them, sure made the Advent calendar bewildering!

Since Advent has a different number of days each year, I've included twenty-eight devotions, plus an extra thrown in for good measure. It's like how, back in my dad's junkyard, we always had a leftover part or three at the end of a rebuild.

So feel free to read at your own pace. You can even skip some entries. Just be sure to read the "Christmas Eve" entry on—you guessed it—Christmas Eve. And maybe save that last piece of chocolate for Christmas Day.

HOW DOES THIS BOOK WORK, ANYWAY?

Each entry will walk us through the very first Advent from Mary and Joseph's everyday, gritty perspective. We often get so caught up in the immensity of Christmas that we overlook the very human story of a pregnant couple taking a road trip. Mary and Joe even have a minivan—okay, it's their donkey, Sully—and they manage to reach Bethlehem without GPS.

There is little known about the days leading up to Bethlehem. Matthew and Luke, the two gospel writers who talk about the birth of Jesus, are stingy with the details. We know angels visit both Mary and Joseph, we know Mary visits her cousin, we know a Roman decree puts the couple on the road to Bethlehem, and we know Jesus has to sleep in a manger because none of the motels have vacancies. Oh, and a bunch of shepherds show up to help celebrate.

But there has to be far, far more to the story. Just because it isn't recorded doesn't mean it didn't happen. These were real people living real lives. So, at times, I'm going to explore what *might* have happened along the way, and you can judge whether it makes any sense. If you disagree with how I portray things—if you think the story probably happened differently—that's okay. Either way, I hope my narrative causes you to think beyond the assumptions (both good and bad) that we usually make about Christmas.

I will also pull in non-Christmas-related scriptures to help us better understand what is happening. Each chapter has a suggested reading, and most of them are directly related to the Christmas story, but every now and then I'll suggest readings from other books, like Romans, Philippians, Timothy, and Micah. I've included two questions and some space at the end of each devotion so you can take notes, process your thoughts, or draw a doodle. My hope is that each entry will give you something interesting and helpful to wrestle with.

One more detail about my writing: I regularly prefer humor to theological orthodoxy, which can get me into trouble. If you tend to read books with your theology filter set to max, you might want to take a deep breath before turning the page—but I hope you do turn the page and give me a chance. Ultimately, my aim is to speak truth in a world starving for authenticity. Just remember that humor is my love language, and I truly love Jesus.

WHAT'S ADVENT, ANYWAY?

Before we start our holy road trip, I want to define Advent. Advent is the Christian season during which we anticipate the arrival of Christ. Strictly speaking, Jesus has already arrived, so we relive the story each year as a reminder of how spectacular the whole thing really is.

As a child, I learned in the Christmas story that Mary was expecting. I heard adults talk about living in expectation. My buddies and I told each other what presents we expected to unwrap. All those different ways of expecting piled together in a confusing jumble. It wasn't until I was older that I realized the jumble was actually the genius of the season. Everything is expecting. Everything is living in anticipation. That's what makes Advent so remarkable.

Advent is so many things rolled into one world-changing event. Advent is preposterously *human*, with a pregnant teenager and a loud cousin and complicated in-laws and a couple trying to make sense of it all, culminating in a messy and exhausting childbirth in a barn (or a cave, or a Motel 6 … don't get picky).

Advent is also preposterously *spiritual*, with unexpected angels, and promises of God showing up to redeem the world, and the Holy Spirit making even the unborn jump and kick for joy, culminating in the birth of a Savior. It is preposterously *personal*, with promises of hope and joy for each of us, culminating in undeserved forgiveness through grace. And it is preposterously *communal*, with families and shepherds and neighborhoods and wise men and nations brought together to learn from and work with each other, culminating in even stronger community bonds.

That's the beauty of Advent. During this season, we live in expectation on every conceivable level— and even some levels we can't conceive of.

The first Advent changed everything, and I believe every Advent since has had a chance to do the same. So if you're ready, we'll start our road trip tomorrow. Imagine, if you will, the moment Mary realizes exactly what the angel has just told her and shouts, "Wait, what?!?!?"

The Freaked-Out Teenager

Luke 1:26-38

Do not be afraid, Mary; you have found favor with God. You will conceive and give birth to a son, and you are to call him Jesus.
(vv30-31)

The human side of Advent begins with a teenage girl.

Have you spent much time around teenagers? I've parented two and founded a ministry that works with hundreds. When describing teenagers, "rational" isn't at the top of my list. When I was a teenager, I worked in my dad's junkyard, and most of my acts of irrationality shall remain secret.

Still, God chose to send an angel to Mary when she was a teenager. And that angel announced that Mary was special (always a good way to start a conversation with a teen), Mary had no reason to be afraid (not sure she believed that, but let's continue), and Mary was pregnant.

"Oh, okay, I'm cool," Mary must've said to herself, "and I don't have to worry, and I'm ... wait, what?!?!?"

Picture Mary's response: eyes widening, cheeks reddening, breath coming in stops and starts. Mary stares at the angel, mouth agape, mind running through all the possibilities, and then mumbles, "That's not how Mom explained it would happen!"

Next, Mary does the obvious thing and asks the angel, "How in the name of the Big Guy Above is this possible?"

Being the mouthpiece of God, the angel gives what appears to be exactly the answer Mary needs to hear, because she responds simply, "I am the Lord's servant … may it be to me as you have said."

In other words, "Pregnant? By the Holy Spirit? To bear the savior of the world? Okay, bring it."

Now, let's be honest: how does Mary not still have a million questions and emotions? I can't imagine a teenager saying something so calm at such a moment.

So maybe Mary reacted as I would have. Maybe she freaked out, argued with the angel, or refused to believe what she was hearing. Maybe—like old Scrooge—she blamed it on a piece of undigested meat. The story in Luke 1 lacks a lot of detail, and it seems reasonable to think a teenager didn't *only* fold her hands and sweetly accept the angel's word.

On the other hand, maybe she did! Maybe she was that extraordinary. Maybe she was chosen to be the mother of God for that very reason.

It's possible Advent begins with a freaked-out teenager coming to terms with the best-planned "unplanned" pregnancy in history. But also, Mary models how we can rise above our boorish human instinct to deny, scoff, and dismiss.

What if embracing the anticipation of this Advent season really is as easy as Mary makes it seem?

This Advent, what might you do if someone tells you to expect the unexpected?

How might you embrace the anticipation?

Um … Mom, Dad? We Need To Talk!

Mark 9:14-29

***Immediately the boy's father exclaimed, "I do believe; help me
overcome my unbelief!" (v 24)***

Today's gospel reading veers away from the Christmas story because we need to recognize the difficulty Mary must have had simply believing what was happening. There had to be a moment or three when she prayed much the same thing, saying, "I do believe … help my unbelief."

Some like to imagine that after the angel's visit, Mary understands and accepts everything that's about to happen. She's an unmarried, pregnant teenager living in a patriarchal society … and somehow she still enjoys God's full blessing. Everything looks rosy for her, and now she can get on with living a peaceful, blessed life.

Or not. If we were in Mary's place, even if we were mature enough to handle such news, wouldn't we still feel the need to process what had happened with someone? Our reaction today would likely be to text our closest friends: "You are not going to believe what just happened to me! OMG!" (I'd throw in an angel emoji for good measure.)

Mary definitely had to tell her parents, too, which doesn't sound like fun. For anyone. Whenever and however it happened, it had to be hard. Think about the courage required for Mary to relay the story. It took real guts.

Then picture her parents' reaction: shock and confusion for sure, but also—make no mistake—doubt about the details. Imagine their subtle glances as they listened to Mary's story. The questions they must have had about her fiancé Joseph. Their raised eyebrows as Mary claimed the whole pregnancy was being orchestrated by God.

It's possible Mary's parents never really believed her. It's also possible they did, of course, but what would *you* say if your teenage daughter told you a tale like Mary's?

This is a lot like the story in today's gospel reading. The father wants to believe, but he just can't muster the faith to do so. Jesus challenges him, and the father responds with an extraordinary request, saying, "I believe; help me overcome my unbelief!"

Sense the anticipation in his plea. This father has been waiting for years for someone to cure his son. Now he dares to hope that this is the moment. He's living in anticipation, but he's still in need of help. He can't get there on his own.

I wonder if Mary's parents felt much the same. They probably wanted to believe their daughter, but wow, this was a tough one!

No matter how we read this story, one thing is clear: Mary's parents raised an amazing young woman who could handle what was being asked of her. Reading between the lines (always dangerous, but fun), I wonder if her parents were more concerned with her faith, strength, and courage than with her reputation. Or, for that matter, their own.

My guess is that, at the moment of truth, when all their fears and hopes and beliefs came crashing together, their default mode was to love their daughter.

This Advent season, what seems too difficult to believe?

And how might you, even in the midst of unbelief, choose to love those around you?

The Loudmouth Cousin

Luke 1:39-45

When Elizabeth heard Mary's greeting, the baby leaped in her womb, and Elizabeth was filled with the Holy Spirit. (v 41)

Like most teenagers, Mary needs to talk with someone who isn't a parent. Her best friend Susie down the road? Bad idea, because then the whole neighborhood will know about the pregnancy. Her school counselor? Budget cuts eliminated the position. The local rabbi? Maybe, but then again, telling him she's the mother of the Messiah seems like a bit much.

Instead, Mary heads off to visit her cousin, Elizabeth. Older and more like an aunt, Elizabeth will be the perfect listening ear. She'll offer stability and comfort. Plus, her husband has already met an angel, so there's a good chance she'll believe Mary.

But I doubt Mary expected the greeting she got!

Poor Mary just wants to disappear and find a little sanity, but when she arrives in Judea, her older cousin shouts, loud enough for every neighbor to hear, "BLESSED IS THE CHILD YOU BEAR!"

Mary is probably blushing and thinking, *Well dang, now the whole freakin' world knows I'm pregnant!* (Of course, she didn't think "dang" because, well, she's the mother of God. And I'm doubtful about "freakin'" as well. Scholars debate this point. But still.)

By this time in the story, Mary has already gone through a lot. So I'm guessing something sneaks into whatever weird mix of emotions she's experiencing.

Doubt.

Yes, I said it. We all have doubts from time to time. It's a perfectly natural human reaction, even for Mary, the mother of God. *I can tell the pregnancy is real, but was the angel? Is this actually a God thing? Can I trust what I've been told?*

Elizabeth, however, is brimming with certainty. After letting the neighbors know Mary is pregnant, Elizabeth shouts, "BLESSED IS SHE WHO HAS BELIEVED THAT WHAT THE LORD HAS SAID TO HER WILL BE ACCOMPLISHED!"

Elizabeth has zero doubts. She senses what is happening. So does her own unborn child, who leaps in her womb. (He grows up to be John the Baptist, by the way.)

Something unique is happening. Something of God.

When Mary shows up with doubts, she's greeted by a loud, loving cousin whose excitement brings a rush of confidence.

Advent is a season of anticipation, yes. But make no mistake: it's also a season to take a long, hard look at our doubts. We all have them. We may bury or ignore them or spout platitudes as answers to them, but we all have doubts.

Which is why, this season, we all need an Elizabeth in our lives.

This Advent, who is the wonderful, loudmouth, faith-filled person who loves you through your doubts?

And how are you that person for someone else?

A Stiff Drink At The Local Tavern

Matthew 1:18-25

Joseph son of David, do not be afraid. (v 20)

While Mary was coming to terms with her role as the mother of Jesus, another drama was taking place across town.

Even though the Bible doesn't say exactly *how* Joseph learned his fiancé was pregnant, he definitely found out at some point. Since he was a standup guy, he decided to end the relationship quietly: no need to hurt Mary or make her life any harder than it was.

I'm sure the news sent shockwaves through the families. Joseph's parents must have learned about Mary's child as well. I wonder if Joseph brought it up during an awkward pause at the dinner table. Or maybe Mary's parents dropped by to privately reveal the details over baklava.

"So good to see you! We brought snacks," said Mary's mom, stepping inside.

"Got any decent wine?" Mary's dad asked with a sigh. "We're gonna need it."

Or maybe Joseph's parents weren't in the loop at all, and his future father-in-law took Joseph out for a drink at the local tavern. "Well, you see, Joe, man to man, it's like this … um … hey, maybe we should order drinks first. Do you like bourbon? Beer? Vodka! Yeah, you need vodka. Trust me on this."

However the news broke, Joseph figured the honorable thing was to split up with Mary. "Pregnant by the Holy Spirit" was a few steps beyond his ability to comprehend.

Until one night, after deciding to end the engagement, he unwittingly attended one of the most dramatic reveal parties in history … though scholars still debate whether the angel actually glowed baby blue.

But I'm getting ahead of the story. Like a Hollywood plot, an angel appeared to Joe at just the right time and told him, "Suck it up, buttercup." Wait, no, the angel didn't say that exactly. The angel said, "Don't be afraid," which is kind of the same thing.

Mary's child, the angel told Joseph (in so many words), was going to be the hope of the nation. And Joseph didn't have to be afraid because God was at work. In fact, it was Joseph's time to step up and be brave—to love Mary as he should since she was carrying the child who would bring salvation to the world.

No pressure or anything!

Few of us live at the pivot points of history. Even fewer of us have the courage to meet the moment. Joseph did both, and the world changed forever. Today, we are blessed because of him.

This Advent season, are you anticipating difficult conversations?

Will you hide from them, hoping to divorce quietly from the pain? Or will you bravely lean into them?

The Confused Couple

Mark 1:1-8

And so John the Baptist appeared in the wilderness, preaching a
baptism of repentance for the forgiveness of sins. (v 4)

Today's reading may come as a surprise since, on the surface, John the Baptist doesn't have a whole lot to do with Advent. Or does he?

Have you ever wondered about the first moment Mary and Joseph talked about what was happening? They had to, right? Everything was so momentous, so surprising, and they really only had each other to confide in. There are a zillion unrecorded details (scholars debate the exact number, some saying it's only a few billion) about this singular moment … and even Matthew and Luke leave us in the dark.

So I'll use my common sense (and some wild guesses) to fill in the blanks. Maybe it went something like this.

"So … " Joe begins, looking away, "you're pregnant?"

21

"Yes," Mary answers, looking right at Joseph, "but by the Holy Spirit."

Joe nods his head, then looks at her and says, "Yep, that matches what the angel told me."

Mary's eyes bug. "Wait—*you* saw an angel too?"

"In a dream. He called me a buttercup and told me to suck it up. To be brave."

Mary nods her head. Risks a smile and says, "I'm glad you know. And that you're here."

"Me too."

Cue the soundtrack and a sunset.

Of course we don't know what Mary and Joseph really said, but they must have swapped stories about their remarkable situation. They probably expressed a mixture of fear and hope. I'm sure they made plans. They worried and dreamed. In some ways, they were like every other couple who discovers they are pregnant. They had to adapt and figure out what to do next.

At some point, though, they must have realized they could talk forever and still fail to comprehend. At some point, they must have sat in silence, holding hands and reflecting on what it all meant and what they still didn't understand.

Maybe quiet moments like that—times when there is nothing to say, and all we can do is marvel—are part of what God is calling us to this Advent.

Of course, as we saw with Mary and Elizabeth, there are also times when your loudmouth cousin gets involved. For Jesus, thirty years after his birth, that loudmouth cousin was John the Baptist. Like Jesus, John's coming had been foretold for hundreds of years, and when he appeared on the scene, he instantly became *the* guy to listen to.

While Matthew and Luke give us some details about the birth of Jesus, Mark and John skip straight to his adult ministry. In Mark, the story opens with John the Baptist acting as the circus ringmaster, announcing the next act is going to be unforgettable.

Advent can be complicated. We discover moments for grand pronouncements alongside moments for quiet reflection.

Perhaps we need both to live in true anticipation.

Have you made the time to simply marvel at the extraordinary story of Advent?

What might your prayer be during such a time?

Lights, Advent, Action!

John 1:1-18

The true light that gives light to everyone was coming into the world. (v 9)

Mark begins his gospel by introducing John the Baptist, then jumps directly into the adult ministry of Jesus, skipping right past a good three decades of events, including the "Christmas story." Interestingly, while this season looms huge in our minds, the New Testament writings about it are fairly brief.

Today, we read the opening to John's gospel and notice something similar. John introduces Jesus as the cosmos-creating Word rather than a baby. No fully occupied inn, no angels explaining things to confused humans, no manger, and definitely no plastic trees at Walmart covered in fake snow. It's like John didn't even know about Christmas!

Still, the gospels of Mark and John are filled with a sense of eager anticipation, even without shepherds and wise men. When we read the first chapter of John carefully, we see birth, change, and hope. The true light is coming, as a human, and he is going to change everything.

To show this, John fills his gospel with beautiful imagery. A professor of mine once challenged us to discover all the times John uses "light" as a theme ... and it's a lot!

Not coincidentally, Advent is a season of light breaking into darkness.

We string lights on every surface: houses, trees, lampposts, cars, and even pets. In my hometown, a locally famous guy uses 600,000 lights to decorate the exterior of his home! People drive from all over the region to see the display, like wise men following a star.

Advent is also a season of spiritual light, though this light has yet to fully arrive. There is a duality here (another theme in John). Something brand new is coming, and we live in anticipation. Like switching on a light bulb in a dark room, we are going to see new things. Our old and worn ideas will be replaced. The fears hiding in the dark recess of our hearts will be exposed, and any darkness in our souls will be driven away.

When the true light arrives, the beauty of the world will be revealed.

On one level, we string up Christmas lights (even 600,000 of them) because we love a show. On another level, we celebrate with lights because we are living in hope. We want to celebrate, even as we embrace the utterly unfathomable illogic of God becoming a newborn human.

The Gospel of John doesn't give us traditional details about the birth of Jesus, and yet its opening few verses lay the foundation for hope. John challenges us to understand that living in anticipation is to live in the light. And when we live in the light, we cannot help but spread it from heart to heart to heart.

This Advent season, are you living in darkness? How so?

Do you know someone who needs a glimpse of true light in the midst of darkness?

Sully And The Road Trip

Luke 2:1-7

So Joseph also went up from the town of Nazareth in Galilee to Judea, to Bethlehem the town of David, because he belonged to the house and line of David. He went there to register with Mary, who was pledged to be married to him and was expecting a child. (vv 4-5)

For Joseph, it's another long day at work. Now he's not just saving money for himself and Mary, but for the baby, too. He arrives home, covered in sawdust (or maybe stone dust), and greets Mary. Despite being in her third trimester, she's been working hard to get their home ready for the baby. She's perpetually tired, and this whole "mother of the Son of God" thing has lost its appeal.

Then the news hits: the Romans require them to make a 90-mile journey by donkey for the privilege of paying more taxes.

I doubt Joseph's response was, "C'mon, honey, this'll be a fun road trip!"

And Mary had to be thinking, "Seriously, a road trip? On a donkey? While pregnant? No way."

Besides the difficult travel, the forced trip will likely mean a missed paycheck or three, plus expenses that aren't in their budget. Traveling half the length of the country will expose them to the elements, robbers, surge pricing from unscrupulous hotel operators, and security lines staffed with extra-grumpy TSA officers.

Okay, maybe not that last part. But Mary and Joseph don't have any option besides complying. Arguing with the Romans isn't a wise life choice. So, despite every reason not to, they pack up Sully the donkey and head south on Highway 777. Even though she's pregnant with the Son of God, Mary finds herself swaying toward a distant town where she doesn't know a single soul.

Theirs is a story of waiting, of anticipating, within a larger story of waiting and anticipating.

Advent inside Advent. As soon as Mary and Joseph start their road trip toward Bethlehem, they can't wait to arrive … even though the journey will be exhausting and they have no idea what will happen to them when they get there.

We might feel the same way this Advent. It's a wonderful season, but it can be draining. Sometimes, we want to move past the hard stuff as quickly as possible or even skip straight to the end.

But like Mary and Joseph, we can't really know how life is going to turn out. All we can do is continue the journey in faith.

Do you feel a lack of clarity about what you want or need this Advent?

Can you identify with taking a difficult journey with an uncertain end?

Did You Remember To Pack The Goat Jerky?

Mark 6:7-13

These were his instructions: "Take nothing for the journey except a staff—no bread, no bag, no money in your belts. Wear sandals but not an extra shirt." (vv 8-9)

Wondering what today's passage has to do with Advent? Hang in there and I'll try to explain.

As I wrote in the introduction, there isn't a lot known about the days leading up to the donkey ride to Jerusalem:

> *But there has to be far, far more to the story. Just because it isn't recorded doesn't mean it didn't happen. These were real people living real lives. So, at times, I'm going to explore what might have happened along the way, and you can judge whether it makes any sense.*

33

Today is a great example. What do all of us do before a trip? We pack! (But if the Spirit moves you … does that service include boxes and packing material?)

Joking aside, look at the instructions Jesus gives his disciples in Mark 6. To me they seem less about the exact details and more about beginning the journey in vulnerability, with a willingness to trust along the way. Jesus knows his packing instructions will force his disciples to relate with others, even as they rely on the grace and goodwill of others.

Now I'm sure Joseph and Mary wanted to pack food, money, and an extra shirt or three, not to mention toothbrushes, a coffee maker, sunglasses, the GPS mount for the donkey, sunscreen, duct tape, and a Yelp list of the best ice cream shops along the way … all the basics they needed for a two-week road trip.

But the actual packing had to be complicated. They knew their baby was coming, which meant diapers, blankets, wet wipes, and an educational mobile to hang above his manger. Caring for Sully would mean spare shoes, hay, and plenty of water. Since they didn't have a lot of margin in their budget, they needed to prioritize. And even if they packed perfectly, they'd be gone a long time, so where would they stay along the way?

Tired, confused, and stressed: that's a minefield for a couple. Even a simple question might have set things off.

"Honey, did you remember to pack the goat jerky?"

Cue explosion.

Honestly, though, I expect Joseph and Mary were operating out of trust, both in each other and in God. Even when things were tense, they chose hope over fear. Maybe, miles down the road, they even laughed about the goat jerky fight.

Moments like that are when the sheer joy of Advent can refresh our hearts, minds, and souls. Suddenly we can see past the petty concerns in our lives and ponder the real and lasting hope of the season.

But for those moments to happen, we have to let go of worry, fear, and sometimes anger. And, in the process, rely on the grace and goodwill of others.

During Advent, we let go because we sense something remarkable, healthy, and loving is about to happen. Even if we forgot to pack the goat jerky.

What do you need to let go of this Advent season? What is stopping you?

Can it be hard for you to "pack light" and be vulnerable as you rely on others?

Did You Unplug The Coffee Pot?

Philippians 3:10-14

Not that I have already obtained all this, or have already arrived at my goal, but I press on … (v 12)

Advent continues as Mary and Joseph's road trip to Bethlehem begins. Obviously, things were different two thousand years ago, but I suspect there were familiar concerns. Did they make it a mile from home before wondering if the coffee pot was unplugged? Had they remembered to ask the neighbors to put out their recycling bin? Had they told the post office to hold the mail until they got home?

They didn't ask those specific questions, of course. Maximus, their Roman mailman, had already told them he'd keep their mail in his chariot until the next time he saw them. (Trust me on this—you don't have to start researching it, okay?) Still, whenever we take a trip, it's human nature to worry about what we may have left undone.

This is actually the opposite of Advent. During Advent, we look forward rather than backward, which is exactly what the Apostle Paul is getting at in today's reading.

37

The future can seem quite distant, whereas the past feels so close. But that's a myth. Of course, if we follow some kind of literal, linear timetable, then yes, yesterday is "closer" than a week from now. But yesterday truly is gone. It exists only in our memories and dirty laundry, both real and metaphorical.

But the future? Oh, the future is coming fast!

I doubt Mary and Joseph spent too much time worrying about the coffee pot. Sure, they probably had a few backward-looking moments. Who wouldn't? But as they began their slow walk to Bethlehem, they soon looked ahead. Filled with curiosity and perhaps a touch of anxiety, if not outright fear, they longed to discover the truth waiting at the end of their journey.

They pressed on, looking forward, because at the center of their hearts burned a sense of anticipation. They were living the first Advent.

This Advent, are you worrying about what you have left undone? It's understandable, but the past is already past.

What are you, or could you be, anticipating? How are you, as Paul writes, pressing on?

What Do You Mean We're Lost?

Luke 19:1-10

For the Son of Man came to seek and to save the lost. (v 10)

The thing about road trips is that you need to get lost at *least* once. If you always know where you are and where you're going, you're not on a road trip—you're commuting!

Nothing is written about Mary and Joseph's road trip to Bethlehem, but I imagine they had a few "polite conversations" about being lost. Remember: they knew their destination, but they didn't know exactly what the journey would bring. Even if they were on the right road, it was still difficult to know how much further it was to the next village, roadside well, or ice cream shop.

Now think about this same scenario spiritually. Getting lost is a very real possibility on a road trip, and that's true in our spiritual journey as well.

The reading today—a fun story about an overeager tax collector—touches on this. Check out what Jesus says to Zacchaeus in verse 10: "For the Son of Man came to seek and to save the lost." I can't help but chuckle at the idea of Mary bringing this up with Joseph amid an argument about which way to go. "Look, I've got the baby Jesus kicking inside me," she says, pointing to her stomach for emphasis, "and he came to save the lost, so turn *here*!"

I bet Joseph didn't argue. And I bet Mary was right: the ice cream shop *was* right around the corner.

This Advent season, we may find ourselves lost at times. And even when we find the path, there's no guarantee we won't get lost again.

The good news is that, like Mary and Joseph, we know our destination. And every time we are lost, we will be found by the One who came to save.

Every Advent is new. We know the final outcome—Immanuel, God with us—but there's no road map for how we get there. That's scary but also exciting. May this year's Advent take us on a new and refreshing journey.

At this point on the journey, do you feel lost or on track?

What do you think Jesus means when he declares that he came "to seek and to save the lost"?

Who Is This Child?

Luke 2:25-40

Simeon took him in his arms and praised God ... *(v 28)*

Spoiler alert: don't read today's scripture if you don't know what happens in the Christmas story.

Now that you've been warned, I can tell you that in today's reading, we learn that baby Jesus was, in fact, born!

Sorry to take the suspense away, but it isn't my fault. The good news is right there in Luke 2, delivered by Simeon, a random and righteous citizen of Jerusalem, and an octogenarian named Anna. Just over a week after Jesus is born, Simeon holds the baby and declares that the Messiah has arrived. (He also provides Mary with a foreshadowing of the grief that lies ahead for her.) At the same time, Anna appears, wrapping her ancient arms around the baby and confirming his identity.

This makes me wonder if, weeks before on their journey to Bethlehem, Mary and Joseph speculated about what kind of child was in Mary's womb. *Who is this child?* It's a question every parent asks. Sure, they had the word of visiting angels, Elizabeth, and probably others, but still. *Who is this child, really?*

A child about to be born is in control of nothing. Geographical location, sex, parents, time period in history, genetic predispositions … this kid could be anything. (And, second spoiler alert, this kid turns out to be *everything*.)

When I worked in the junkyard as a kid, we kept a mental list of the cars in the yard, but never their details. If a person asked about a backseat for a Mustang, our best answer was, "A Mustang came in last week; feel free to look." It was a coinflip if they'd return delighted or disappointed.

My point? We couldn't control everything in the junkyard. We operated in a gray zone of "maybe we do, maybe we don't." I think the same is true about what we can and can't control about ourselves.

Curiously, we tend to emphasize the few things we *can* control as sources of our strength. "I worked hard" is a common refrain of the successful—but what about those who worked just as hard or harder, and never achieved that same success? There is so much about our lives that we did not, will not, and cannot control. In many ways, we are the sum of countless decisions other people made. We weren't even consulted!

Mary and Joseph, like any other young parents, had to be thinking along similar lines. *What will happen if we make this decision? Or that one? Will we change who our child turns out to be? And he's the Messiah?!*

It takes courage to admit we can't know all the ramifications of our decisions, just as it does to recognize how much of who we are was never our choice.

Yet understanding this is a step toward humility and authenticity. It's a step toward spiritual and mental health.

It's a step toward God.

And yes, it really helps when someone like Simeon or Anna speaks into your life!

Do you know someone who could use your voice in their life to help them see who they really are?

Given everything we can't control about our lives, what can you focus on during this season of Advent?

I Don't Know

John 20:24-29

Unless I see the nail marks in his hands and put my finger where the nails were, and put my hand into his side, I will not believe. (v 25)

It takes courage to admit we don't have all the answers, especially when we feel lost on our journey.

Wouldn't it be easier if we always knew which way to turn? We long for life to be simple and clear, but it never is … or not for long, anyway. Most days life is messy, and sometimes it's wildly confusing and even exhausting. No wonder we question and doubt.

That's why Thomas joins our Advent readings today. Doubting Thomas is famous for, well, doubting—but he isn't unique in this. Peter expresses doubt when he says he doesn't know Jesus (Luke 22). John the Baptist seeks extra assurance about who Jesus really is (Luke 7). Many other characters in scripture express doubts or admit they don't have all the answers. Swallowing pride can be hard, but it's also an essential part of being human.

I wonder at what point in their journey Mary or Joseph simply and humbly admitted, "I don't know."

Of course, that phrase can take on so many meanings. "I don't know" can be aggressive when we bark it at someone. It can be humble when we seek forgiveness for our earlier arrogance. It can be fun when we say it with a mischievous smile, as if to say we can't wait to find out. It can be resigned when we're ready to admit defeat.

The first Advent must have been filled with many "I don't know" moments. *We* know the story, but Mary and Joseph were living it in realtime. I'm sure parts of it seemed normal, but the rest must have been an incredible, incomprehensible mystery for the young couple. Admitted out loud or not, there was so much they didn't know that we take as obvious today.

At some point, Joseph grudgingly agrees they are lost. At some point, Mary confesses she doesn't fully understand how she is pregnant. Both admit they didn't pack enough diapers. And then, together, they continue on.

"I don't know" moments can both break our pride and begin to heal us. Admitting our doubts can spur growth.

Which, when you think about it, is what Advent is all about.

What "I don't know" thoughts are you wrestling with this Advent?

Is there someone in your life wrestling with doubt? Remember, they may be experiencing a period of growth.

Theology And Christmas Recipes

Matthew 22:34-40 and Micah 6:8

***And what does the Lord require of you? To act justly and to love
mercy and to walk humbly with your God. (Micah 6:8)***

Books about the first Advent often overlook the incredibly human experiences of everyone involved.

On the one hand, theologians are happy to write *ad nauseam* about how Jesus was both fully human and fully divine. On the other hand, more approachable devotions share recipes for Christmas cookies with a Bible verse tacked on.

But beyond theology (which is important) and chocolate chip cookies (which are my favorite), it helps to remember that Mary, on her way to Bethlehem, was nine months pregnant, for gawd's sake! I mean that literally: Mary was pregnant for God's sake.

Whether Mary was riding on Sully the donkey, walking alongside him, or simply trying to rest at the side of the road, she suffered all the physical realities of pregnancy. Her back hurt. Her feet were swollen. Sleep was difficult to come by.

53

Obviously I've never been pregnant, but I'm observant enough to know that most pregnant women aren't in the mood to debate meandering theological rabbit trails. That's why today's readings emphasize the simplicity of faith. Love God. Love your neighbor. Act justly. Love mercy. Walk humbly.

We can over-theologize the Christmas story, just as we can sanitize it with tinsel and Hallmark movies. Each may occasionally have its place, but neither is what Mary experienced.

Like Mary, most of us live in the real world of sweat, sore muscles, and exhaustion. Life is gritty, not unlike a junkyard, and covered in a fine layer of grease and dust.

Pregnancy is never easy, much less in the pre-medicine age of the first century. Somewhere along the road to Bethlehem, Mary simply wanted a glass of cool water and a comfortable place to nap—or maybe a scoop of ice cream. I hope she found what she needed.

Keep the human side of Advent in mind, and embrace it. There are moments of balance between the deep theology of the season and the surface trappings of the season. Trust your body and your heart. Take a nap. Rest in anticipation.

Don't overthink it today. Write something if you want to, but otherwise, just take a deep breath and rest.

Chocolate Chip Cookie Cravings

John 4:1-42

The woman said to him, "Sir, give me this water so that I won't get thirsty and have to keep coming here to draw water." (v 15)

When my wife was pregnant, my renowned chocolate chip cookies were the craving of the moment. Okay, to be fair, I was the one craving them. But I digress.

I wonder what Mary craved. She must have longed for something. Did Joseph stop at Dairy Queen to get her a Bethlehem Blizzard? Or push Sully the donkey a little harder to get to Krispy Kreme while the donuts were still hot?

Look, I know these questions are a bit silly. I'm not asking them to be funny—or not *just* to be funny. My hope is to highlight just how human Mary and Joseph were.

We often imagine the angel-blessed couple gliding effortlessly to Bethlehem, but the truth is far different. Along the way, they were definitely hungry and thirsty, just like the rest of us on a road trip.

This is also true—maybe even more true—of our *spiritual* journey. We can long to satisfy a certain spiritual craving. Scripture, along with many hymns and songs, speaks of hungering and thirsting spiritually.

Today's reading touches on this. The Samaritan woman at the well has an amazing conversation with Jesus. She is clearly craving something, whether it is water, forgiveness, wisdom, or simply being seen. Maybe she really wanted cinnamon rolls! The point is, she seems to have both literal and spiritual cravings that are satisfied by Jesus.

To this day, archaeologists debate what the first-century equivalent to Dairy Queen was, but you can bet Mary asked Joseph to stop at one. And no doubt they had spiritual cravings as well, as they anticipated what would happen next along the journey.

Advent can feel like a journey of perpetual craving. As a season, it might end with the birth of Jesus, but as a practice, it can last a lifetime. An Advent heart lives in ongoing anticipation.

What are you craving physically? Spiritually?

Are you finding moments in the journey to stop and discover delight?

Should We Start A College Fund?

Matthew 6:18-34

*Look at the birds of the air; they do not sow or reap or store away
in barns, and yet your heavenly Father feeds them. Are you not
much more valuable than they? Can any one of you by worrying
add a single hour to your life? (vv 26-27)*

Amid the anticipation, Mary and Joseph had plenty of time to worry as they made their way to Bethlehem—just like we would. "Will we be ready when the baby is born?" they asked each other. "Will the baby be healthy? Will we be good parents? Should we start a college fund?"

Okay, maybe not that last one. But in general, whether two thousand years ago or today, we worry when we think about what might happen in the future. Sometimes we worry a lot.

Wouldn't it be great if we could ignore our worries this season? That doesn't seem possible, though. We can't just tell ourselves we won't worry about feeding the seventeen people coming over for dinner on Christmas Eve.

Instead, what if we actively, ruthlessly attacked worry? I wonder if battling worry might release our hearts and minds to the joy of the season, replacing days and weeks of apprehension.

There's hope in today's reading, even though it has always ruffled my feathers a bit. (And I don't just mean the part about the birds.) At first reading, Jesus's advice feels simplistic. It's like he's saying, "Just don't worry!"

I want to respond, "How?!"

But looking at this passage a bit more deeply starts to answer that question. Jesus tells us that the key to ending worry is to store our treasure in heaven. To open our eyes to truth and light. To serve the only God who loves us. To appreciate the beauty around us, even in the midst of our worries.

This helps, but it's still a work in progress for most of us. I've never quite been able to pull off the "no worries" thing, but I still find myself trying.

I'm sure Mary and Joseph also found moments beyond worry, perhaps when they glimpsed a flock of birds dipping and swirling in the evening air.

Have you ever ruthlessly attacked worry? What was the result?

When it comes to worry, if you feel like a work in progress, focus on that last word: progress.

Oh My God, The Baby Is Kicking!

Philippians 2:5-11

Who, being in very nature God,
did not consider equality with God something to be used to his own advantage;
rather, he made himself nothing
by taking the very nature of a servant … (vv 6-7)

The Advent story is beautiful for how easily we can identify with its real-life situations.

Mary pumps her mother for information on pregnancy and childbirth. Joseph has to figure out how to get time off for an unplanned road trip to Bethlehem. There are visits to relatives, road trips, and roadside motels. This is the stuff of everyday life and, like everyday life, things can get complicated fast.

For instance, can you imagine Mary's reaction the first time she felt Jesus kick? It's a moment shared by all mothers, of course, but I wonder if Mary experienced a unique mixture of emotions. I bet she felt relief: *Phew, baby is doing fine!* Probably shock as well: *Ow! Hey, you're perfect, and perfect babies shouldn't kick their moms!* And there was definitely joy: *Oh my God, the baby is kicking! No, wait, I mean, oh my baby, God is kicking! Um … Jesus is kicking!*

Mary's pregnancy was far from simple. Like any expectant mother, she experienced days of utter joy and fascination, but there would have always been a sense of concern. How could an expectant mother not have a touch of fear about the delivery?

This is a part of Advent we don't often explore because it feels too confusing. Advent is about living in anticipation, yes, but we still need to be honest: what we hope for can also be what we fear.

Mary, an expectant teenager, understood this well. Joseph, the father who wasn't the actual father, also understood. One mystery of Advent is the way many stories become one story and how, even in the midst of fear, goodness can dawn.

Our reading today seems to capture this dichotomy: Jesus is God and Jesus is human. He came as a baby in order to change our entire relationship with God.

Mary didn't know this, but Jesus would come into life as the ultimate junkyard rebuild. He was bits and pieces no one expected to see together. Perfect, yet pooping. All-knowing, yet unable to walk. The savior of the universe, yet wrapped in rags and laid in a feeding trough.

Because Advent encompasses, well, *everything*, it is the season that unifies us. Our fears, our dreams, our hopes … they all become part of the one true story.

That's the beauty, mystery, and depth of Advent.

Are there two things in your life that seem contradictory but are equally true?

Consider what fears might be contained inside your greatest hopes.

Magazines And Yoga

Matthew 2:1-12

After Jesus was born in Bethlehem in Judea, during the time of King Herod, Magi from the east came to Jerusalem and asked, "Where is the one who has been born king of the Jews? We saw his star when it rose and have come to worship him." (vv 1-2)

Remember magazines?

Back in the day, my wife and I subscribed to several. Before a trip, we'd pack any unread magazines, which would begin the journey as a heavy pile that would slowly dwindle as the days passed. Whenever we finished an issue, we would give it to someone, leave it on a lobby table, or toss it in the recycling.

Turning the page (groan) back to today's devotion, I've long pictured Mary riding Sully and reading a magazine while Joseph led them toward Bethlehem. And I can just imagine the ensuing conversation.

"Joe," Mary asks, "have you heard of yoga? All the wise men are talking about it these days. Apparently, there's a class in Bethlehem for expectant mothers. Maybe we should go?"

And Joe, knowing it isn't really a question but rather a statement, responds with a non-question of his own.

"Sounds … fun?"

This is one of my silly made-up stories, yes. But every expectant mother does take steps to prepare for the big day. Maybe it's asking friends and family to help out. Maybe it's stockpiling easy-to-prepare meals. Maybe it's just ordering a few more pillows to make the bed a bit more comfortable.

That's a part of Advent we can overlook. We focus so much on *anticipation* that we forget Advent involves *preparation*. If the only thing we do is prepare, we won't be fully living in the moment—but if all we do is anticipate, we won't be ready when the moment arrives.

The wise men from the east did both. When they saw and understood the heavenly sign, they couldn't wait to visit the person it pointed to. First things first, though: they packed up the minivan with everything they'd need for the long journey. Only then could they fully anticipate a remarkable discovery.

This Advent, you've been anticipating the arrival of Jesus. But what have you done to prepare, in a spiritual sense?

How will your spiritual preparation during this season impact you or others in the months ahead?

You Still Gotta Get The Donkey Fed

John 20:30-31

Jesus performed many other signs in the presence of his disciples, which are not recorded in this book. But these are written that you may believe that Jesus is the Messiah, the Son of God, and that by believing you may have life in his name. (vv 30-31)

Even though we're expecting the birth of Jesus at the end of our journey, today's reading reminds us how much of the story we'll never know. Jesus did and said countless things as an adult that were never written down—and that's doubly true for the events of Advent!

So, unsurprisingly, I'm going to make some guesses about what happens to Mary and Joseph as they leave Nazareth and walk toward Bethlehem. As the days pass, their mood begins to shift from anxiety toward determination. Some of the stuff that felt incomprehensible begins to feel, strangely, both incomprehensible *and* normal.

"We're the parents of the Messiah," muses Joseph, "but he's still gonna need diapers."

"Elizabeth promised to go to Costco for us before we get back from Bethlehem," Mary replies, "which will give me time to put away everything from this road trip."

With every day that passes for Mary and Joseph, life moves forward, and they move with it. Life takes on a rhythm. Not a comfortable rhythm, mind you—have you ever ridden a donkey? In the desert? While pregnant? (Full disclosure: I haven't, but I'm sure it's the exact opposite of comfortable.) Still, they start to take each day as it comes. There are fewer unanswerable questions and more coordinated teamwork each evening as they tether the donkey and start cooking hotdogs.

There is something for us to learn here. We rightly do our best not to let the busyness of the Advent season obscure its real meaning. We light candles to represent hope, peace, joy, and love. We remind ourselves to pause and reflect on the wonder of the season. These are good practices, of course, but Mary and Joseph didn't get the memo.

They needed to get a few more miles down the road. They had to figure out how to stretch their budget after roadside vendors jacked up prices. They prayed that Mary's water didn't break somewhere in the middle of the desert.

No matter what we're anticipating, we still have to-do lists. You still gotta get the donkey fed— especially when it's Sully, who has patiently carried you and your gear all the way from Nazareth. That's life. Finding a rhythm is the key to balancing the power of Advent with the gritty realities of our world.

Is it more natural for you to lean into anticipation or to focus on your to-do list? Why do you think that is?

What are you doing to find a rhythm in this busy season?

Hope Is Invented Every Day

Romans 5:1-5

And hope does not put us to shame, because God's love has been poured out into our hearts through the Holy Spirit, who has been given to us. (v 5)

Our determined couple plods closer to Bethlehem. As they pass various villages and landmarks, they experience different feelings about what is happening to and through them. It's quite a mix of emotions, of course, but at the core is anticipation.

Anticipation is complicated. We can feel a mixture of joy, wonder, fear, excitement, eagerness, heartbreak, and confusion. Underneath all anticipation, though, runs a clear truth: hope is our foundation.

As James Baldwin once said in an interview, "Hope is invented every day."

Hope drives this entire Advent story. Hope that this child is indeed the hope of the world. Hope that this whole journey is part of God's perfect—and perfectly confusing—plan. Hope that all will be well.

Maybe even Mary and Joseph's simple hope that the next place they rest will have a clean bathroom.

Advent is about hope on every level. You want macro-level hope? The Messiah is coming! You want micro-level hope? Joseph will have a son! You want eternal hope? God is setting the stage for saving the entirety of the cosmos! How about simple human hope? Mary is a mother!

Hope drives the Advent story, just as it drives so many of our stories.

I once saw hope with my own eyes in a remote Central American village of refugees. The students in their small school, grades 1-8, had low test scores and high dropout rates. One day an organization offered high school scholarships to the 8th graders with the best test scores. Few students ever managed to attend high school, so this was a big deal.

A year later, when I visited again, scores had gone way up. Attendance was up. Engagement was up. Kids were smiling more. Before the scholarships, nearly every student had no hope of continuing on to high school, so what was the point of trying?

But now? Now there was hope, and it was motivating the entire school.

This year, let's take time to reflect on the hope of Advent. I wonder how its power will change us.

Do you feel a foundation of hope this Advent season? If not, what is getting in the way?

How can you invent hope every day?

Carrying God's Love

John 15:9-17

***As the Father has loved me, so have I loved you … I have told
you this so that my joy may be in you and that your joy may be
complete. (vv 9, 11)***

Mary and Joseph have been asked to believe a lot of incredible things, but as they pass Jerusalem on their way to Bethlehem, I suspect one claim might have jumped to the top of the list: that their baby would rule Israel.

The angel, after giving Mary a horror-movie jump scare, had been pretty specific, telling her, "The Lord God will give him the throne of his father David, and he will reign over Jacob's descendants forever; his kingdom will never end" (Luke 1:32-33).

David's throne was Jerusalem, the most important and powerful city for a good long way in any direction—and at the moment it was being ruled by the most important and powerful empire in the world. As the couple stared in awe at the mighty walls surrounding the city, the notion that the baby in Mary's belly would be Jerusalem's king might have seemed too bizarre to believe.

And not just at the how-will-baby-Jesus-kick-out-the-Roman-army level. Look at Jesus's parents: a teenage girl and a blue-collar laborer from a backwater town. Their kid will work the family business, not become a king. That sort of thing only happens in fairy tales!

Yet the angel had told them exactly that. Mary and Joseph knew their scriptures and understood the prophecies. If this child was indeed the Messiah, then his sweep would be global. Israel was only the first step. Jesus, due any day now, would change the world.

In the moments they allowed themselves to dream, that prophecy had to be utterly mind-blowing. Imagine the excitement! Imagine, as parents, the joy!

Looking back, we know the life of the Messiah shocked everyone. After Jesus was born, his family was forced to become refugees. Upon returning to Nazareth, he learned a trade, then quit the family business to become an itinerant teacher and healer. His ministry was so successful (and angered so many people) that he was crucified like a criminal. This would have been the end of the story, except he rose from the dead and returned to heaven, proving he was exactly who he said he was all along: God, the Messiah.

With a resume like that, it's no wonder Jesus's story spread across the world like wildfire. And everywhere it sparked, joy followed. Forgiveness, freedom, and love flourished.

The link between joy and love is inescapable in today's reading. Read it a few times and you'll see it shining through. Joy comes from loving others. Joy comes from accepting God's love. Joy comes from friendships centered on love.

As Mary and Joseph looked at Jerusalem, I wonder how big their dreams were for Jesus. King? Maybe. Universe changer? Maybe … and maybe not. I suspect it was impossible for them to dream that big— just like I suspect *we* don't dream big enough about Jesus, either.

I do believe Mary and Joseph were living in joy, though. How could they not? Not only were they surrounded by God's love, Mary literally carried God's love.

This Advent, as you wait in anticipation, how might you embrace joy?

We read about hope being invented every day. How might joy also be invented every day?

What Do You Mean You Didn't Reserve A Room?

Luke 2:7

... there was no guest room available for them. (v 7)

With Jerusalem in the rearview mirror, Mary and Joseph can see Bethlehem.

Finally, Mary thinks.

Her journey from Nazareth has been exhausting. Never mind her pregnancy—a gritty road trip isn't exactly her dream vacation.

Soon, the couple is through the gates, and Mary sees a welcoming neon sign.

BETHLEHEM BED & BREAKFAST
WELCOME TAXPAYERS!
FREE WI-FI AND HEATED POOL

I don't care which room we're in, Mary thinks. *All I want to do is take off my sandals and lie down.*

"Joe, once we're checked in, would you mind popping over to the Kwik-E-Mart and grabbing some chocolate chip cookies?" Mary asks, climbing down and taking Sully's halter.

"Sure thing, babe," he responds, heading inside, "back in a minute."

Many minutes later, Mary is still outside, shifting back and forth on her feet. Sully gives a tired sigh, then glances meaningfully at the all-you-can-eat hay in the stables, so Mary pulls a dried apple out of the saddle bag for him.

When Joseph eventually comes out of the revolving door, Mary can tell something isn't right. He isn't looking at her, and his fists are clenched.

"Joe?"

"They—" he starts. He shakes his head like a dog, blinks, and finally looks at her. "Mary … they don't have a room for us."

There it is. Mary and her baby need a room, stat—but there isn't one.

Road trips can hold surprises like that. Often, nobody is to blame, but when you're tired, disappointed, and frightened, surprises can trigger pent-up frustrations. Mary and Joseph have finally arrived in Bethlehem … but have they really arrived if they have no place to stay?

Advent can feel like that for us, too. We eagerly anticipate the arrival, only to find out the arrival isn't quite ready for us.

And we have no idea what will happen when we finally do arrive.

We've all experienced last-minute disappointments. How can you keep past disappointments from robbing you of joyful expectations this Advent?

When God surprises you with a last-minute change in plans, how do you tend to cope? What can you do now to prepare?

Frantically Searching

John 21:1-19

When they had finished eating, Jesus said to Simon Peter, "Simon
son of John, do you love me more than these?"
"Yes, Lord," he said, "you know that I love you."
Jesus said, "Feed my lambs."
(v 15)

Joseph scratches his beard. *This is bad*, he thinks. *Really bad.*

In the hour since the innkeeper turned them away, he's been searching frantically for another place to stay.

He looks at Mary, who is resting in the shade by a well and chatting up a local. He frantically tweaks a few more filters on the hotel app. One-star and up? Check. Price range increased to maximum? Check. Amenities? Every single one, unchecked. And still, the closest available place is a two-day walk and costs more than he makes in a week.

Mary catches his eye and asks an unspoken question. He shakes his head, then fires up the app for the fifth time.

It must have been wildly frustrating. Their baby will arrive any minute. *The* baby, as Mary and Joseph know—but to everyone else in Bethlehem, they're just another poor, pregnant couple amid a sea of grumpy travelers.

I wonder if Joseph was tempted to pull rank with an innkeeper. "My wife is nine months pregnant, sir, and do you know who with? The Son of God, who is the Messiah and the King of Israel. You're saying you don't have room for the *Messiah*? Wait … hang on! Come back!"

There's no way Joseph actually tried that. How could he? Even if he fully believed it himself, nobody else would have—not to mention the danger of declaring your unborn baby as the King of the Jews in Roman territory.

And so Mary and Joseph remain in limbo. No baby yet, nowhere to stay, and no clear plan. Which, in a way, is where Peter finds himself in today's reading. The story is longer than most, but it reads like a scene from a movie, so I hope you savor it.

Jesus surprises his friends by helping them catch far too many fish and then cooking breakfast on the beach. As the meal ends, Jesus speaks with Peter, and the subtext is obvious: Peter's recent denial of Jesus. Against all odds—never tell Jesus the odds—Peter's betrayal becomes the ground where the seed of reconciliation is planted. Rather than shaming Peter, Jesus calls him to an even deeper love, to a way to move forward in generosity and service.

Jesus has reason to hold a grudge against Peter, but, as always, he chooses love. He even cooks breakfast.

Something tells me Mary and Joseph choose love as well. Yes, the baby is almost here, and yes, they have nowhere to stay. But even as they are stuck in limbo, I suspect they operate in love, by faith, and in anticipation of something incredible.

As Advent moves toward something incredible, how are you choosing to respond to disappointments?

If you wronged someone, would you expect them to cook you breakfast? What does that teach us about grace and love?

Can't We Just Go Home?

Luke 2:14

Glory to God in the highest heaven, and on earth peace to those on whom his favor rests. (v 14)

We've been dancing around the "no room at the inn" crisis because we know how the story ends. In the moment, however, the pressure on Joseph and Mary to get a roof over their heads must have felt crushing.

Imagine the scene. Mary, the ready-to-give-birth teenager, sits uncomfortably beside the road. She scrubs a few tears away, streaking her dirty cheeks. Joseph, the worried road-tripper and expectant father, stands beside her. He wipes a few tears of his own. Worry, fatigue, frustration, and fear mark their faces. Countless people stream past, barely glancing at the couple. Sully, always a patient traveler, munches grass beneath a tree. *My humans look like they need to catch a break*, he thinks.

Mary takes a long breath that turns into a sigh. So does Joseph. Or maybe their sighs are a silent prayer. *Why us, Lord? Why this?*

Most of us can relate. We've had similar moments. Sometimes, life becomes too much, and all we can think about is finding an escape. *What will happen to my family if I don't get this job? How can I possibly parent my difficult child? Why do my parents seem to be aging so quickly?*

In other words, "Why us, Lord? Why this?"

I'm sure Mary and Joseph had moments when they wished they could run back to Nazareth and pretend the angels had never appeared to them. And yet, somehow, I think they chose to cling to a deep sense of peace amid the chaos. The question "Why us, Lord?" actually had an answer: because God had chosen them. That knowledge was their refuge in the storm.

As today's reading promises, Jesus bestows God's peace on those he loves. (Spoiler alert: that's everyone!) This doesn't mean we won't endure seasons of pain, fear, suffering, and worry. Mary, although she was carrying the Prince of Peace, still experienced all of that, so it's certain we will as well. However, in the midst of any circumstance, God makes a deep and lasting peace possible.

Perhaps we will never completely understand things from our human perspective, but as the angel said to the shepherds, "Do not be afraid. I bring you good news that will cause great joy for all the people. Today in the town of David a Savior has been born to you" (Luke 2:10-11).

What in your life is making you ask God, "Why me? Why this?"

In the midst of that, what can you do to cling to God's lasting peace this season?

We Could Use Some Lysol

Matthew 8:5-13

When Jesus heard this, he was amazed and said to those following him, "Truly I tell you, I have not found anyone in Israel with such great faith. (v 10)

Mary and Joseph finally catch a break. To their shock, someone steps out of the passing crowd and asks, "Are you the couple looking for a room?"

We aren't told who plays that part. It could have been a sympathetic innkeeper or a kind farmer. It could have been a friendly local or an angelic being disguised as a human. We don't even know if Mary and Joseph were sitting on the side of the road … they might have knocked on a hundred doors until they found the answer they were looking for behind the hundred-and-first.

At some point, however, someone made the offer. "Look, it's not much, but you're welcome to stay in our stable."

Whoever that person was, God bless them for their small act of generosity. It's unnamed people like this in the Bible who often capture my imagination. Later in Jesus's life, someone offered him a colt to ride for his triumphal entry into Jerusalem, and someone else provided a room for Jesus and his disciples to gather for their last meal together.

And what a welcome surprise the stable was for Joseph and Mary! They must have been equally thrilled and relieved by the unexpected good news.

We're always on the lookout for that. In today's reading, for example, Jesus is astonished by the faith of a Centurion. I enjoy this story, in part because it's so fun to picture Jesus being surprised. He always seems to know everything and everyone, but here we have a plot twist: Jesus is "amazed" by what he sees!

Mary and Joseph, so tired and alone, had to be amazed as well when they reached the stable. Of course, I'm sure they were none too pleased about the mice, the dust, and the animals, not to mention the odor. Let's just say Mary sent Joe out to pick up some Lysol and a pooper scooper.

Still, it was a start. And after everything they'd endured, the stable was amazing … especially for Sully.

Both spiritually and literally, what amazes you right now?

Ask God to put a small act of generosity on your heart during this Advent season.

Silent Night It Ain't

Matthew 21:12-17

He overturned the tables of the money changers and the benches of those selling doves. (v 12b)

The scene is set for a Hallmark Christmas.

Inside the picturesque stable, adorable sheep and goats rest meekly beside a manger filled with fresh straw. In the background, camels stoically chew their cuds. The teenage mother-to-be is resting comfortably. Joseph, calm and confident, smiles at Mary. She reaches out a hand, and he takes it. "This is perfect," she says, placing her other hand on her swollen belly. "Everything is exactly how I pictured it would be."

Um … no.

My family moved to a small ranch when I was twelve, so I know a bit about the inside of barns and corrals. The sheep make a racket, the goats butt heads, the camels pass gas—we had cows, but close enough—and mice, rats, fleas, ticks, and spiders have the run of the place. Plus every creature is pooping and peeing, 24/7.

Essentially, Jesus was born in a junkyard without the wrecked cars. Our Christmas stories often sanitize a situation that was messy, active, noisy, and smelly. In our search for *Silent Night*, we overemphasize peace and quiet. It's a wonderful song, but the idealism is unobtainable. I'm sure there were moments of tranquility during the birth of Jesus, but they must have been brief, and surrounded by chaos.

Today's reading is about an especially chaotic moment in Jesus's adult ministry. He enters the temple courts and discovers unscrupulous salesmen are ripping off poor religious pilgrims. Responding angrily, Jesus destroys the crooks' tables and chases the men out the door. In that moment, Jesus didn't simply embrace chaos … he created it!

Advent—the real story, not the Hallmark version—contains a healthy amount of chaos. Real people in difficult situations are forced to choose between fear and doing amazing things, even when they're scared. Let's embrace the grittiness of Mary and Joseph, and honor them for dealing with the sheer madness of it all.

Are you more comfortable with Silent Night or flipping over tables? Why do you think that is?

In moments of madness this Advent season, remind yourself that chaos can sometimes be positive. How can you find the meaning of Advent in the chaos?

Hurry Up And Wait

Luke 2:41-52

After three days they found him in the temple courts, sitting among the teachers, listening to them and asking them questions. (v 46)

Most of us are terrible at waiting. We change lanes on the freeway to get a few seconds ahead, we analyze grocery store checkout lines, and we stare at our phones when we have no other way to pass the time. If waiting is a spiritual discipline, most of us suck at it.

Sometimes, though, we have no choice but to wait … and that can be a marvelous experience.

Advent is about living in expectation. It's about waiting. And on this day, some 2,000 years ago, Mary and Joseph sat in a stable, waiting for several things.

Maybe for a room to open in the inn so they could leave the stable and finally take showers.

Maybe for a Roman bureaucrat to give them official permission to head back to Nazareth.

Definitely for the baby to arrive.

In these moments of waiting, Mary and Joseph talk. They dream. At night, they go out into the cool air and stargaze. Maybe they see something new in the night sky: a bright star they'd never noticed before. Something big is about to happen.

The birth of Jesus and the new era he is promised to bring might be beyond their minds' ability to understand, but it is not beyond their hearts' capacity to sense.

Jesus knew how to wait. Today's reading is about the time he was left behind on a road trip, and it took his parents half a week to find him. He waited in the Temple and used the time wisely, listening and talking to the older teachers day after day. Perhaps he asked them questions that shaped how he understood his own future. We don't know exactly what happened, but we know that Jesus grew in wisdom and favor, both with God and his fellow humans.

Mary and Joseph had to learn what it meant to wait, and their son soon learned the same.

And so, during Advent, we wait as well.

You're going to wait for a lot of things this Advent. What can you do to use the time wisely?

Are there any dreams that feel too big to comprehend but that your heart still senses?

Christmas Eve

John 16:20-22

Very truly I tell you, you will weep and mourn while the world rejoices. You will grieve, but your grief will turn to joy. (v 20)

The time for waiting is over. The baby is most definitely on the way!

Joseph pings the family text chain and then calls the hospital, which assures him a bed is waiting for Mary. Their go bag is already packed, so Joe straps it to Sully, who clip-clops his hooves to show how ready he is. The miniature (and incredibly safe) baby saddle is a bit harder for Joe to figure out, but after a few well-timed movements from Sully, that gets strapped on as well.

It's the moment Mary and Joseph have been longing for and fearing at the same time, simultaneously frightening, exhilarating, hopeful, and confounding. This complexity had to be even more pronounced for Mary, who was far from her familial support system. (Nothing against Joe here, but it's hard to imagine him being as much help as Mary's mom and her cousin Elizabeth.)

Jesus is arriving, and it is in these moments of holy revelation that Mary cries out—in fear and pain, yes, but also in fierce joy. Her cries are prayers asking for God's help. I almost wrote that they were prayers asking for God's presence, but, well, that's exactly the point. God is already present.

I do wonder if there were some humorous moments. At some point, Mary's face is contorted in pain as she shouts at Joseph, "You are never touching me again!"

To which he meekly responds, "Honey … I never *did* touch you!"

That's probably not what happened, but it makes me smile. And it makes the whole story so *human*.

Jesus reminds us in today's reading that childbirth is a time of intense pain and amazing joy. The two coexist, sometimes blending into one another. As Tolkien writes in *On Fairy-Stories*, there is a "joy beyond the walls of the world, poignant as grief."

Both joy and grief cut sharply into our souls, it's true, but Advent reminds us that the order matters. The grief of this life reminds us of something deeper and stronger, hinted at in childbirth: an eternal joy that can never be stolen.

Have you had moments when you had to live through pain to find joy? What did you learn?

Why are joy and pain so intimately connected?

God Is With Us

John 13:34-35

*A new command I give you: Love one another. As I have loved you,
so you must love one another. By this everyone will know that you
are my disciples, if you love one another. (vv 34-35)*

Merry Christmas, friends.

Our journey has reached its end, and today we proclaim: Immanuel is here!

Immanuel, meaning "God with us." It's a truth that is staggering, and staggeringly beautiful.

The wait is over. The Messiah has arrived as a crying, pooping, vulnerable baby. He is wrapped in cloth and placed in a manger previously used by donkeys, goats, and camels. Yet even in this humble beginning, we can shout, "God is with us!" In fact, we know God is with us *because* of this humble beginning.

A week and a half ago, I mentioned the four candles of Advent that traditionally represent hope, peace, joy, and love. I suspect that if Jesus had a favorite candle, it would be that last one. In today's reading, he gives his followers a new commandment.

Love one another.

And not just that, but love one another in the *same way* Jesus loves.

Advent reminds us what that love looks like: becoming vulnerable in order to love more perfectly. None of us can do that exactly like Jesus did, but we're still commanded to try.

Ultimately, that's what we anticipate during Advent: the arrival of Love. In fact, that's what we anticipate for all of our days. It's how the world can change, how we can be reconciled to all things, and how we can hang on to hope, cultivate peace, and share joy.

So, let's live in anticipation of love—now, until the end of our days, and always.

I know today is a busy day, but take a final moment to reflect. Even if you only have thirty extra seconds, that's fine. First, appreciate this simple and life-changing truth: God is with us.

Next, follow this short exercise by reading the phrase four times, emphasizing the bold word each time.

God is with us.
God **is** with us.
God is **with** us.
God is with **us**.

Finally, rest in this reality: God is with us. Immanuel. Amen.

Our Road Trip Is Over

Luke 2:1-20

Let's go to Bethlehem and see this thing that has happened, which the Lord has told us about. (v 15)

Our Advent journey has reached its end.

The stars of the show, Mary and Joseph, have gone from angelic announcements to an uncomfortable engagement to an epic road trip to Bethlehem, and now they are the parents of Jesus. It's been quite an excursion!

And, of course, the journey is not complete. Advent continues for each of us. With a blend of hope and fear—and some healthy irreverence at times—we wait for what's next.

As we end this season, we have time for one last fun story. It's the evening after the birth of Jesus. Mary is exhausted. When she and the baby finally fall asleep, Joe asks Sully to watch over them while he goes outside to take some calming breaths in the night air. The animals in the stable continue to eat and poop and make all sorts of noises.

Cue the arrival of a bunch of stinky shepherds, who stumble into the stable, eager to test with their own eyes whether the terrifying angels they saw in the skies were right.

Sure enough, there he is, just like the angels announced: the Savior!

Their shouts of great joy wake Mary and the baby, of course. Mary could do without the gaggle of strangers surrounding her and the baby. She wonders if they at least brought some ice cream, but all they have to offer is wonder and worship. But Mary, being the mother of God and all, is patient. She knows her child is the hope of the universe. Why not let a few poor shepherds see Jesus, even if he's crying? It'll be another memory for her to cherish.

Today's reading shares Luke's version of this story. I encourage you to read it out loud—and bonus points if you can sound like Linus in *A Charlie Brown Christmas* from 1965. (Double bonus points if you drop your blanket when you say, "Fear not!")

May each of us reject fear, embrace love, and encounter the same Hope the shepherds longed to see.

Merry Christmas!

Confessions

Most books have an acknowledgments page because even the most narcissistic authors don't want to look like jerks. I confess it's easy for me to consider this "my" book, but it's not—it's our book. And that's why I'm calling this section *Confessions*.

I confess to using a collaborative writer. Some people call them ghostwriters, though I don't think David has ever written a ghost story. He's helped me since my professional writing began, laughing at my bad jokes, making my stories better than they deserve, and helping me sound more like *me*. He's a colleague, but more importantly, he is a friend. Thank you, David.

I confess to having the equivalent of a middle schooler's grasp of grammar. (Some say humor, too, but that's a different confession.) My personal assistant, Anne Stoneberger, has edited every word of this book twice, at least. She puts the apostrophes in the right places and buys commas by the truckload to make me look smart.

I confess to being taken completely by surprise at the tens of thousands of readers who signed up for my daily email devotions. The marketing gurus at Parable Group kept growing the list faster than I could write flippant things that made people unsubscribe. Many thanks to Greg Squires, Laura Clark, and the Parable team for making that happen.

I confess to being flabbergasted that people actually liked those email devotions. The goal was to write a non-theologian's take on familiar Bible stories and make them short, funny, and real, with a touch of snark. I confess to pushing the edge and admit it was sometimes hilarious when feathers were ruffled. But most loved it. So thank you, readers … without your encouragement this book would not have been published.

I confess to being lazy and not wanting to write another book, but Jeannie Bruenning at A Silver Thread encouraged me. She was willing to handle the publishing work I didn't want to do and suggested a streamlined process that wouldn't disrupt my life. Thanks, Jeannie.

I confess to wondering why I bother writing at all when I could be spending time with my wife, watching a sunset, and sipping from a glass of good wine with our golden retrievers at our feet. Thank you, D'Aun, for supporting me in this Junkyard Wisdom™ hobby!

Finally, I confess to feeling a sense of loss. My mother, Dee Goble, passed away last year at the age of ninety-nine. She was—and still is—the inspiration for my faith journey.

At the same time, I confess to a sense of unsurpassed joy at the birth of my first granddaughter. This book is dedicated to Lily; I know Dee would have loved her.

Roy Goble
Northern California
August, 2024

The Guy Behind The Grit

Roy Goble grew up working in his family's junkyard. To this day, he sometimes sees life through a lens covered in grime and grit.

He has run a family-owned real estate investment company for more than four decades. He co-founded the educational nonprofit PathLight International, has served on nonprofit and academic boards, and authored two other books about generosity and leadership.

Over the years Roy has been called both a troublemaker and a peacemaker, often at the same time. He's a three on the Enneagram, so he's shooting for a higher score next time. Roy is easily bribed with Napa Cabernet Sauvignon, dad jokes, and pictures of golden retrievers. (He has two golden retrievers, Sammie and Holly.)

Roy is married to his high school sweetheart, D'Aun. They have two adult children, one son-in-law, and one incredibly cute granddaughter. Oh, and two hilarious miniature donkeys named Sully and Indy.

Go to junkyardwisdom.com to sign up and stay in touch, or email Roy directly at roy@junkyardwisdom.com.

The Guy Who Helps Roy with Words and Stuff

D. R. Jacobsen holds a BA in English from Westmont College, an MA in theology from Regent College, and an MFA in creative writing from Seattle Pacific University. As David Jacobsen, he is the author of Rookie Dad: Thoughts on First-Time Fatherhood. He and his wife live in Central Oregon. When not thinking about words, he likes to hit the trail with his golden retriever and root for the Timbers. Connect with him at jacobsenwriting.com.

www.ingramcontent.com/pod-product-compliance
Lightning Source LLC
Chambersburg PA
CBHW060802150426
42813CB00059B/2852